# DAD'S GUIDE
## SHOOT 5
## YELL FORE
## WRITE ③

BY GERARD ECKER

# FREE

## Book

**Unlock Your Free Bonus Book!**

As a heartfelt **thank you** for choosing our book, we're delighted to offer you a **FREE** book.

To my dad, the master storyteller of the greens, whose hilarious golf stories are as legendary as his love for the game. This book is inspired by your unbeatable tales and the laughter we've shared on and off the course. Thank you for every laugh, every lesson, and every "creative" golf rule. May we continue to share smiles and stories for many rounds to come.

Oliver couldn't sleep. He lay awake with anticipation. Tomorrow he was golfing with his dad for the first time! "Dad's stories make him sound like a golf superhero. I can't wait to see him in action," Oliver thought, excitement dancing in his mind.

At breakfast, Dad told Oliver exciting stories about his adventures playing golf. "My golf game is so good, even the birds stop to watch me tee off! Especially the eagles." Dad said jokingly. Oliver laughed, picturing birds perched on the trees, admiring Dad's golf skills.

"I hope I'm as good as him someday." Oliver thought.

Oliver and Dad prepared to tee off on the first hole. "Watch me, Oliver!" Dad exclaimed as he swung his club with all his might. But the ball veered off to the side, whizzing past a squirrel and heading toward another group of golfers.

"Fore!" Dad yelled loudly.

Oliver looked puzzled. "Dad, why do you yell random numbers when you hit the ball? Does it help?"

Dad chuckled and explained, "Oh, Oliver, 'Fore' isn't just a random number. It's a golf term as old as the game itself. It warns people that a ball is headed their way."

Oliver laughed, "So it's like saying 'Watch out!' but in golf language?"

Dad nodded, "Exactly! If you yell 'watch out' on a golf course, people will look at you funny!"

When Dad's next shot disappeared into the woods, he and Oliver embarked on a woodland adventure to find it. The ball had bounced off several trees like a pinball so finding it seemed nearly impossible.

"Found it!" shouted Dad, slipping a ball from his pocket onto the ground. "Sometimes, you just get lucky."
A few steps behind, Oliver held back a laugh, pretending to not see the ball "magically" appear on the forest floor.

As they reached the second green, Dad's ball was quite far from the hole. "In golf, we have something called 'gimmes'," Dad explained, picking up his ball. "Gimmes are when you pick up the ball because you would've made the putt anyway. It helps keep the game moving smoothly."

Dad had missed a putt from closer than this on the first hole, but the wheels began turning in Oliver's head. He imagined all the times where he could use "Gimmes" in his life. Like on his upcoming spelling test! "Close enough!" he thought.

On a tricky hole, Dad stood at the tee, aiming his club carefully. "Watch me, Oliver," he said with a big smile. But when Dad swung, the ball didn't go where he wanted. It flew out of bounds!

Dad laughed and said, "Oops! Let's pretend that didn't happen with a mulligan."

Oliver, eyes wide with curiosity, asked, "What's a mulligan, Dad?"

Dad grinned, "A mulligan is just a fancy word for a do-over. In golf, we sometimes get a second chance to make a better shot."

Oliver's eyes lit up with excitement. "Wow, Dad! I need mulligans in my life! Like when I spill juice on my shirt or when I forget to clean my room!"

Dad chuckled, "That would be pretty handy, wouldn't it?"

Oliver nodded, still grinning, "There's no chance Mom would go for that!"

On a short Par 3, Dad's ball headed straight for a pond. With wide eyes, Dad exclaimed, "Oh no, it's heading for the water!" But then he grinned and said, "Wait, I think I saw it skip across!" Oliver, was certain he saw the ball make a splash, but when they got closer, Dad found another ball nearby and pretended that it was his.

"What luck!" Dad chuckled, looking pleased with himself. Oliver couldn't help but giggle at Dad's clever trick.

As they played on, Oliver noticed Dad's scorecard at the 7th hole. Something seemed funny about the numbers. Oliver knew Dad was good at math, so he was puzzled. "Did Dad write down a 3 instead of a 5?" Oliver wondered. Then he realized, "Dad's not just playing golf; he's also playing with the numbers!" Oliver smiled at Dad's inventiveness, understanding that his dad sometimes made the game more fun by bending the rules a little.

Reaching the ninth hole, Oliver's curiosity bubbled over. "Dad, are these all official golf rules?" he asked, trying to hide his giggles. Dad joined in the laughter, "I may have bent a couple rules to impress you. Okay, more than a couple." Dad admitted.

"I should've set a better example. The heart of golf—and life—is honesty. It's more important to play fair and enjoy our time together than to worry about the score," he added.

As they put away their clubs, Oliver looked up at his dad with a grin. "Dad, today was super fun. Maybe you... I mean we... should get some golf lessons," he suggested. "Then you wouldn't need to use those funny rules so much."

"You're right, Oliver. I think that's a great idea—for more laughs and even better shots," he replied. Together, they left, their hearts light with the joy of the day and excited for their next golf adventure.

Made in the USA
Monee, IL
16 December 2024